"What are we gonna eat?"

Gnat Feathers & Butterfly Wings

by Carla M. Cherry

===== THE SECOND EDITION =====

iiPUBLISHING

Gnat Feather and Butterly Wings
Copyright © 2021 by Carla M. Cherry

Second Edition

Copyright notice
All rights reserved. No part of this book may be reproduced in any form or by any electronic or mechanical means, including information storage and retrieval systems, without permission in writing from the author or publisher, except for the use of brief quotations in a book review.

Cover design by tonii

ISBN: 978-1-7362167-5-0

Printed in the United States of America

iiPUBLISHING
New York, NY
www.toniiinc.com

Dedication

I would like to express my love and gratitude to my teachers, especially, Mrs. Harriet Pine, my second-grade teacher, who first told me I could write. Cecily Parks read the several drafts and encouraged me to push my imagery. Colum McCann, in his Short Story course, told me to push myself and not to give up after reading my short story "The Caretaker's Daughter." Jason Schneiderman and Matthew Lippman, my poetry instructors at Gotham Writers Workshop provided me with a forum to workshop several of my poems. Thank you Matt, for telling me that my words "sing." Sheree Renee Thomas, my Creative Writing teacher from the Frederick Douglass Creative Arts Center, assigned me with writing a tall tale, which planted the seed for "Mama Afrika." Jacqueline Johnson, my poetry instructor from F.D.C.A.C., helped me to fine-tune "Still".

Much peace and love to my friends, especially:

Tanya and Terrence, for always cheering me on, encouraging me to make use of my intellect, and helping me to cope with the loss of my father. Iveliz, for helping me to break out of my shell and taking me shopping. Patrick, Raynard, and Algernon; great Morehouse Men who have always been there. Zakeha, who heartens me by pursuing her dreams.

My Family, especially, my parents Melvin and Paula Cherry. Mommy, you have saved my life, time and time again. I remain in awe of your quiet strength. You are my biggest hero. Daddy, you always wanted me to write, and Donna, thank you helping me format this manuscript. This is for you. My cousin Eric McPherson, a brilliant drummer who is dedicated to his art. My cousin Kiameshia and her children Nasif, Nailah, Yusef Geronimo, Freedom, and Naimah bring me joy and laughter. My aunt Laverne, cousins Jenny and Vivian are three women who inspire. Uncle Bobby, I strive to do with words what you do with your art. My son Khari who has enriched my life in too many ways to explain. My niece Anike, who lights up the world. To the memories of my cousin Ivy and my sister Donna, who always made me laugh and listened when I cried.

To My Ancestors, without whom I would not exist:

Melvin Cherry (father)
Sallie Cherry (paternal grandmother)
Boston Cherry (paternal grandfather)
Pauline Ballew (maternal grandmother)
Robert Ballew (maternal grandfather)
Don Meredith Ballew (maternal uncle)
James Reginald Ballew (maternal uncle)
Ralph Eugene Ballew (maternal uncle)
Robert Maurice Ballew (maternal uncle)
Aunt Bernice Ballew (maternal aunt)
Caroline Cherry Chance (paternal aunt)
Beatrice Cherry (paternal aunt)
Joan Cherry Turner (paternal aunt)
Marguerite Newman (maternal aunt)
Saundra Laverne McPherson (cousin)
Dorothy Daly (paternal aunt)
Milton Council (cousin)

Foreword

Gnat Feathers and Butterfly Wings was my first book of poetry, and it was comprised of poems written from 1990 through 2007. I self-published the first edition of *Gnat Feathers and Butterfly Wings* through Wasteland Press in 2008. I am extremely grateful to Wasteland's owner and president, Timothy Veeley, who formatted the manuscript and designed the beautiful cover art for my first edition; I will always be proud of it.

I am grateful to iiPublishing for allowing me to transition from self-publishing to traditional publication. Although multiple things changed in my life in the twelve years between the first and this second edition—most prominently, losing my cousin Ivy, my sister Donna, and Uncle Bobby—the poems I wrote still ring true, and other than some minor edits, the poems have been left intact. I added several newer poems:
"You Gambled", "African Beauties" and "Sunset" because they suited this collection.

I

Prayer	1
The Reason Why	2
WHERE I'M FROM	4
My Mother Gave Me The World	9

II

Apotheosis	12
To Ida Wells Barnett	17
Progress	18
Nostalgia	20
Mama Wit	22
Ab Intra	26
In a City of Unsurpassed Beauty	30
A Love Poem	32
For Bessie Smith at the Apollo	34
Still	36
The Audition	38
Rerun	40
Legend	44
Devotion	46
Dear President Bush	49
Footnotes	50
Spleen and Sawdust	52

54	For Viola Liuzzo
59	Shelwanda Riley
60	Beauty and Movement
63	A Sonnet
65	Yon Desod
66	The Human Knot
70	If New York Could Talk
72	The Rush
74	Utopia
77	Untitled

III

80	Nom
84	For Grandma Ballew
86	For Aunt Marguerite
88	Black Pearl
94	Daddy
98	Potpourri
100	For Aunt Joan
104	Last Request
106	African Beauties
109	Spring
110	Bits and Pieces

IV

Elusive I	119
The Human Manifesto	120
Honesty	122
Testimony	125
Work in Progress	126
In the Light	128
Confessions	130
A Sestina	132
Dear Sir	135
Biorhythm	136
Simplicity	139
Cacoethes	140
Pulchritude	142
A Period Piece	146

V

The Invitation	153
Troubled Mind	154
Sweet Georgia Brown	156
Ineptitude	158
Resurrection of a Poet	160
Thabiti	163
A Senryu	165
A Deux	166

168	Victim
170	Myopia: A Pantoum
172	A Song For You
175	Beatitude
177	Anike
179	The Anteroom
181	Baggage Claim

VI

184	Fortune Cookie
188	Solitude
189	Pathways
191	A Woman's Wisdom
193	Truth
194	Homegoing
200	Sunset
205	Southern Lullaby

VII

208	Mama Afrika
219	*Afterword & The Author*

I

Prayer

God
please grant this poet
talent
to spin straw words
into gold
as I pour my soul
onto the page.

The Reason Why

Words danced in my head,
taunted like
a little sister,
to let them out to play.

Obliging,
I built skeletons
of poems.

Over the years,
I've dressed them.
One might be too long,
another too short,
too tight,
the color scheme wrong,
so, I picked them clean,
and there they hung,
in a closet.

Sometimes
late at night,
I heard them rattling
to pull them out and
give them their flesh.

One day
the noise
gave me a headache
so
I yanked
my courage
out of its corner.

I kept prying my poems.
When I found pearls,
I polished them with a soft cloth,
strung them together.

Here they are, dressed in their Sunday best.
I hope there will be the
gentle fluttering of my pages,
followed by applause.

WHERE I'M FROM
(A Girly Rap)

Who-ah
Who-ah
Who thinks they bad?

I do!

Who-ah
Who-ah
Who thinks they bad!

I do!

I think I'm bad
'cause Carla's my name
I am so fly
and love is my game

Mmph!
She thinks she bad!

Correction! I know I'm bad!

Mmph!
She thinks she fine!
Fine enough to blow your mind!

Not slim
not short
don't smoke Newport

Look good
smell sweet
my thoughts
are deep.

Tease me
I'll snap on you all day
I joke, I laugh
but I don't play

I teach
I write
If pushed
I'll fight
with words
then fists
if they insist.
Yes!
I am the one
Let me tell you where I'm from!

I am from
Peggie and Boston who survived and thrived after slavery.
I am from their son John
who married Lula
who begot Boston, who married Sallie
and their son Melvin.

I am from
Harriet and Stephen Bates' daughter Florence
who married Milton and had Pauline
who married Robert and their daughter Paula, who married Melvin.

I am from the Bronx:
towering trees that gave us shade when it rained on our games
throwing rocks into Goose Bay, that sometimes smelled of dead fish
best friends Niecy and Tonya from across the way
red-stained fingers holding Chinese apples
(pomegranates for the uninitiated, ya'll)
vanilla cones with rainbow sprinkles from

Marcy's Mister Softee ice cream truck
playing spades
jumping Double-dutch
chalk-stained concrete blocks for hopscotch
bikes rounding corners
handball games that were for me, hit and miss

I am from hip hop
weekends dancing in front of my stereo
index finger poised on pause, making
mix tapes from Mister Magic and Kool DJ Red Alert
and everybody laughing when I
was poppin', lockin', trying to breakdance.

I am from fried onions and croquettes,
collard greens and candied yams,
Great Northern beans with relish and hot water bread,
macaroni and cheese,
Aunt Verne's corn pudding.
I am from "because I said so",
"I don't care if Moses himself said to do it",
"you are because we are, therefore, you will be",
"if you have a friend keep him so, let him not your secrets know".

I am from P.S. 160 and May festivals,
Mrs. Pine, my second-grade teacher who nurtured my poetic soul,
and dried my tears on the last day of school.

I am from I.S. 180 where I played the flute,
helped classmates cheat on Mr. Russo's science tests,
sneaked upstairs to run from security guards at lunch,
lusted after Lee jeans, Izod shirts, matching Pumas

sheepskin coats, name chains and name rings.
I am from Truman High School, where I
skipped lunch, ate dollar Kit Kats instead,
laughed at Mr. Van Deuren's
"when we last left our hero" in biology,
and Mrs. Schraier's funny jokes in Spanish.

I am from Bronx Science
where everyone else was smarter than me
but I learned how to learn
reading and rereading,
scribbling notes in margins and asking questions.

I am from Abyssinian
baptism when I was 19,
communions I've taken since.

I am from longings for love,
motherhood,
Khari's goofy laughter, inquisitiveness,
loving heart.

I wonder
what he will make of this
predilection
of human beings to
create
reflect
struggle
err
and love.

My Mother Gave Me the World

When I was a girl
my mother sat me on her lap
her fingers covering, then
uncovering, syllabic formations,
her voice charming me into understanding.

Before I fell asleep each night
underneath one of the afghans she knitted
she bathed me with Ivory soap
rubbed me down with glycerin
and rose water,
then
words were fanciful stories.

When she arose each day
my mother folded twilight in her hands
and tickled me awake
to face the magic of morning.

Knowing it is the nature of youth
to abhor the necessity of
waiting
as she baked
she always let me
lick the bowl.

As I've been pricked by life's nettles
she has always been there
to soothe.

Every time
I read a book,
write a poem,
rejuvenate,
I thank God
for her.
My mother gave me
the world.

II

Apotheosis

I. A Wondering
What caught my eye was his white shirt,
"My Favorite Heroes Always Kill Cowboys".
I said, "I like your shirt". Beguiled by his
hazel brown eyes I asked, "Which nation are you from?"
He smiled. "Mohawk". We were steps from
the roaring rapids of the Niagara,
and, considering its allochthonous
ownership, I wondered at his calm as
he crafts and sells his jewelry--feathered dream
catchers, silver bracelets, and earrings
featuring kelly-green and turquoise stones.
America and Canada profit,
tourists gawk and take photographs, and they
think about reservations only when hungry.
Sloganed T-shirts never win wars.

II. Truth
I thought of my Mohawk brother when I,
euphoric from my boat ride under the
Falls, heard about the legend of the Maid
of the Mist. A Native American village,
plagued by a wicked serpent god with drought
and death who rejected their offerings of flowers
and fruit. The village allowed a lovely
maiden, Lelawala, bedecked in doe-skin robe
with woodland flowered wreath, and in
a birchbark canoe, to throw herself down
the river, in sacrifice to the god
of Thunder Hunim/He-No.

As a descendant of stolen people,
I strive to glean colored truths from white lies.

That tale sprung out from the
imagination of a European anthropologist.
The Iroquois people have no concept of vengeful gods
and no tradition of human sacrifice.
Weary of Europeans kneading and
rolling their stories like dough, Iroquois
leaders roared like the Mighty Falls, and the
Maid of the Mist boat company had to
apologize. They stopped telling the tale.

The real version from the Six Nations is
that Lelawala, who lost three husbands,
blamed herself. When she canoed down the Falls,
the Thunder gods rescued her. Finding the
evil snakelike creature infecting her,
she was healed in a hidden cave,
and was returned to her people, whole.
She found love again,
and raised a family.

III. Post-Script

I wonder if, one night, a maiden had
a premonition. Her people's beloved Ongiarra wore
a caconym, Niagara. The Confederacy
was Six Nations strong, but the French and the
British and Americans would claim the
land and Falls. Southward, the Seminoles lost
Florida. The Trail of Tears was littered
with bodies. At Wounded Knee, raven black
hair became flying wind as women and
children fled the exploding bullets that
pierced ghost dance shirts. Mournful Native
American children, their hair language,
and culture cut short, in white schools.
COINTELPRO, taking deadly shots at
A.I.M. The braves, no longer counting coup were
building casinos, hoping to recoup
lost wealth. Upon her awakening, she
dipped her hands in her
beloved Ongiarra, and believing
she tasted tears, she set her kayak down
in the rushing rapids allowing it
to carry her, with arms outstretched, to the…

…edge of the precipice.

To Ida Wells Barnett

Beloved Iola
if you could
swoop down
and carry us away
where is it
that you would land?

PROGRESS?

Lost languages
Forgotten rituals
Souls stolen in chains.
Black woes.

Middle Passage
Feeding sharks
Splintered bones litter the Atlantic's bottom
Black woes.

Work
Rape
Birthing
Bleeding
Whippings
Work
Seethings
Work
Running
Hiding
Caught
Slow dying.
Black woes

Freedom
Finally
Sharecropping
Lynching
Cast-away books in packed rooms
Opportunities denied,
Black poverty decried
Black woes.

Marching,
Singing,
Agitating, then
Triumph

Open doors that some won't walk through.
Black woes.

Nostalgia

Nigger
Master raping black women
Ignoring their pleas

Nigger
Black children on the auction block,
Parents on their knees.

Nigger
Eyes averted, whip strikes a slave's back

Nigger
Black man running
Hound dogs sniffing out his tracks

Nigger
White woman points finger at black man
Then, he is well hung, from a tree

Nigger
White bigots snapping pictures
Snatching body parts with impunity.

Nigger
Docile fool with buck eyes
And asinine grin

Nigger
Black man wants respect,
Patience wearing thin.

Nigger
David Walker makes his appeal.
Black defiance, once again revealed.

Despite our racial misery
Houston, Woodson, and the like reclaimed
our lost and forgotten history.

And still
Dudes hug street corners
Sling "niggers" at each other
like bullets.

Even academics use
Nigger
In the context
Of "brotherly love".

If your eyes are blue
and your skin is white,
if nigger slips from your lips,
it's a stick of dynamite.

Fists tense.
Daggers in the eyes.
Anger erupts.
Punches fly.

Nigger
Reeking rotting refuse.
A shackle on the black man's neck.

Nigger
A chain around the brain.
Draining black people of self-respect.

Mama Wit

Those of us who are black
don't have time
to be laying up on somebody's couch
telling our life stories
and singing the blues
about oppression, or
how we wished he or she
or mom and dad had time to spend
or loved us
and cryin' about stress on the job
or that the boss just don't understand
or about the kids
who want and need and cry and fight and hurt and
love us or hate us to death.

Neither can we talk about how trapped we are
in our marriages or unhealthy relationships

Nor can we waste time talking to Dr. Ruth
about our empty or too-full sex lives

God forbid
if you're raped
by someone you once knew
had blood ties to
or even had the bad luck to be caught by
and need to deal with that.

Shit

Black folks got too much to do
and struggle with
and too little money
to be spending time
laying on a couch
talking about our negative thoughts.

We have our sister-friends—
straight from the hip—
our boys to shoot the breeze with
and ourselves.

                              Isn't that enough?

Uncle Don, Donna, and me

Ab Intra

Uncle Don--
my sister's namesake--
handsome
the color of cashews
who
bounced us on his lap
stealthily crept up behind us,
and blew air up our backs just to see us giggle.

I used to stand underneath his chin
his prickly beard grazing my hair
aftershave filling my nose
and his chuckle tickling my ears.

On November 15, 1983
when I was twelve
and home with my father and sister
the phone rang
on the other end
was Grandma moaning and Mommy's frantic sobbing
asking for my father
I stood there attempting to read Daddy's unreadable face
he asked if Mommy had called 911 and swiftly left the house.

When
Mommy asked Uncle Don
are you OK
he only replied,
"I'm just tired, I'm going to take a shower."

Anger turned inward was Untruth

he went into his room
and when they heard the pop
Grandma and Mommy looked at each other
knowing
they ran into his room
and found him
bleeding from his head,
dead at 39.

November 15, 1983
the day anger turned inward was the bullet in a gun.

The suicide note left only instructions--
no life support,
send Carla and Donna to college,

no explanations
about complex sociocultural triggers
fatherlessness
childhood poverty
a woman's wrong
job-related stress
money
a chemical imbalance
or all the above.

If depression is anger turned inward,
then suicide is tragedy turned inside out.

Grandma, left to mop up the sea of blood and brain
from her youngest son's bedroom floor.

Mommy floated through the first few days
tranquilized
after the initial tears
her therapy was her busy life
sunrise to sunset to deep night
getting us up and off to school
herself to work
cooking, cleaning, checking on Grandma
putting up the Christmas tree and gifts underneath.

One night I found her
silently rocking in the recliner,
undulating tears
blue
green
red
lights
illuminating her face.

All we have left of Uncle Don
are ashes,
mementos,
photographs.

And Mommy abhors
locked doors.

In a City of Unsurpassed Beauty

if he were alive what kind of poem
would Paul Laurence Dunbar write
about the Florida housing project
bearing his name
loitering drug dealers and fatherless sons
hovering flies over dirty diapers
assaults and burglaries
nightly gunfire
and an eight-year-old witness to a murder

what kind of poem
would Dunbar write
about a gang of youth who broke
into a woman's home there
each took their turn raping her
compelled her twelve-year-old son to watch
then made her perform oral sex on him,
recorded it on their cell phones

forced her and her son to lie naked in a tub
poured household chemicals over them
burning her skin and his eyes
beat them with a broom and a gun
threatened to set them on fire if they called for help

what kind of poem would Dunbar write about
fear
neighbors closing their ears to her screams through paper-thin walls
and mother and son's mile long walk in the dark
to the hospital

what would Dunbar say to honor Citoya Greenwood, who
speaks up and out
at meetings
and in the paper
"just stop by and see what goes on there",
or to the neighbor
saying to the media,
"so a lady was raped, big deal
there is too much other crime happening here"

what kind of poem would Dunbar write

A Love Poem

Until we find the love

(not sweet sweaty sodic love)

but the love that
had us walk for miles and years and across states
for sold away husbands or wives or children,

kept our elderly at their windows
watching the children and telling on them
for those first and second-hand whippings,

had our men dressed and pressed and
shaking hands on Sundays
'cause these days I'm mostly bumping hips in the pews,

made boys and men remove their hats when
they came courting
(what happened to first date flowers);

Until we find the love that

will make our children stop scowling,
acting out and sexing,

will keep our women partnered
our children with fathers at home
and out of the poverty-prison-industrial complex,

the Red, The Black, and The Green will fly at half-mast.

For Bessie Smith at the Apollo

Put away that paper bag
It's only good for carryin' stuff
All my life, black's put down
And I've had enough

....

Yeah, this chorus girl here
is a deep killer brown
But if she don't go on,
I won't stick around.

....

Go on, dim them lights
I'll sing my blue-black songs
But if this girl ain't on the stage
The show will not go on.

....

....*And I've had enough*

....*I won't stick around.*

....*The show will not go on.*

Still
A Bop
(for G.N.)

Our black blossoms are waiting and wanting.
Someone told one of my girls she's cute,
even though she's dark. Fearing
sepia-toned reflections, she shuns sunlight.
How many of us
look at our kin, and say you're pretty
even though you're light-skinned?

....

when women want to impress
they put on that little Black dress.
Fertile earth is a deep rich brown.
Nina Simone sauntered stages
loving every inch
of her cocoa-sweet skin.
In Song of Songs, Sheba is black and comely.

....

God's gonna cut him down.
Swathe your walls in
dark, dusky
Alek Wek black beauty for
Imani and Aaliyah and Takara.
Our black blossoms are waiting and wanting,

....

.... *So go tell that long-tongue liar*

.... *So go tell that long-tongue liar*

.... *So go tell that long-tongue liar.*

The Audition

the way
she grasped
the pole
with both hands

pushing

and

pulling

and

writhing

her brown loveliness

betrayed
the innocence of her face.

There was no music playing.

Gyrating her hips, expertly

winding her legs

moving in ways I cannot.

She seems to have no audience
except for me.

I am repulsed as I,
rubbernecked,
cannot turn away.

I try to scold her with my eyes.

Hers are askance.

I do not speak,
as it is inherently dangerous
to implore
this stranger's daughter

who
can't be more
than six

to

stop

her

mother

enraptured by oblivion,
is standing right next to her.

When the crowd in the subway car thins out,
she tells her to sit down, and
I,
mother and teacher,
proponent of the proverbial African village,
am absolved.

Rerun

Another black boy, Vaughn Roy,
aged fourteen
on July 10, 2006 was
allegedly beaten
in Brooklyn
with a pipe and epithets
by a gang of white boys
for allegedly looking at a white girl.

Two white boys,
aged fourteen,
were charged with assault.
Three others questioned, then released.
100 Blacks in Law Enforcement
Who Care said
the officers should have
called their supervisors to the scene
and aggressively pursued all the culprits.

Reading the brief story in the news,
I burrowed into my old
cedar trunk, found
my high school varsity jacket
sheathed by buttons screaming slogans:
No justice, no peace
By any means necessary
for Eleanor Bumpers!
Michael Stewart!
Yusef Hawkins!
Yvonne Smallwood!

I checked on my own adolescent son.
Seeing him sleep with his
lengthening brown limbs
splayed across his bed,
I was reassured
by the steady rise and fall of his breath.
I wrapped the jacket around his shoulders.

I've been searching the papers.
Wanna sign up for the next protest.
I have seen nothing yet, except
brief bemused images of young Mr. Roy
and his mother,
confused about why the police
refused to call it a hate crime.

Maybe it's because
Vaughn only needed fifteen stitches
to heal his wounds.

His eyes weren't gouged out
thirty teeth extracted
his ear cut off
wire wrapped around his neck
discarded in the bottom of a river
and funeralized with his distended
bloated face
on display for weeping,
fainting thousands
like another fourteen-year-old black boy
from Up South
fifty years ago.

I'm baffled by hearing more
about Mo'Nique
being escorted off an airplane
for allegedly getting neck-rollin' loud,
and United Airlines being deluged
by phone calls of protest
than I did about this black boy
beaten in Brooklyn.
Perhaps we're suffering battle fatigue—
Restless Leg Syndrome from all the marching,
arthritis from carrying placards,
voices gone hoarse for
Amadou Diallo,
Patrick Dorismond.

We've traded our picket signs for
picket fences
and while our wealth is well-earned
a boy was beaten in Brooklyn for being black.

Legend

Sometimes I sit with
Tupac Resurrection
in my lap
like a family photo album.

In my favorite picture
he is grinning wide,
jumping off a jungle gym.
Had I been there, I would have
chased him
pulled on his shirt
so he'd look at me with those
long-lashed dusky eyes
and after we played a game of tag,
I would ask to meet his mother
to ask if he could come to my house
in the Bronx
to ride bikes
sneak down to the bay
throw rocks in the water
swap *Ebony Jr.* magazines
black history books and
stories about Black Panthers,
listen to the radio
and make up raps.
I know Daddy would have loved
having the kinds of talks
fathers don't have with their daughters
and when Troubles came
Tupac could have spent the night with us.

Our 36th birthdays approach.
I caress the outline of his
triumphant smile
and Thug Life tattoo—
The Hate yoU Gave Little Infants Fucks Everyone
with my fingers.
I wonder
if his father had
willingly wrapped
Black loving arms around him
and this black boy
who loved Shakespeare
had safe spaces to be
would this black rose
who grew from concrete
have been in Vegas
watching black fists
pound black flesh
black sweat
draw red blood, and
after one black fist was held in the air victorious,
Tupac, and
his black fists
pounded black flesh
black sweat
then
black fingers pulled a black trigger
four bullets
rending his black flesh
right, writing hand
right chest
cutting off his black breath
and after seven days,
his death.

Devotion
A Tercet

With bowed head and lowered eyes
Pastor said,
Are there any words for God?

In my pew
With bowed head and lowered eyes
I thought, Yes.

Father, Thank you for waking me up this morning.
Thank you for the breath of life that moves through me.
Thank you for my eyes that can see.

Thank you for my ears that can hear.
Hands that touch,
and the Love my heart feels.

Thank you for my livelihood,
the home that keeps me and mine safe.
Thank you for the food which sustains us.

Thank you for the strength of my ancestors,
their courage in the face of injustice,
and the blessings that we descendants enjoy.

Father, we've listened to our parents--
Degrees from good schools, good jobs, living good lives.
And yet, Lord, it is not enough.

Lord, as a black mother,
I need to know how I can protect my son
since these earthly laws don't keep us safe.

Sean Bell was celebrating his upcoming wedding.
Police fired 50 bullets at him and his friends. He was only 23.
His two daughters lost their father, and his fiancée, her husband.

Kathryn Johnson, sore afraid of the violence on her Atlanta block,
armed herself with her .38 in the middle of the night
when men busted down her door with their no-knock warrant.

She got off one shot, hitting no one.
Police fired 39 times
at this 92-year-old woman.

An officer handcuffed her, and while she lay bleeding,
he planted three bags of marijuana in her basement, and told
an informant to lie about buying drugs in her house.

Lord, we've been praying and singing hymns 400 years
and through our nonviolent resistance lost
Medgar
Malcolm
and Martin.

Lord, the Good Book says, "Thou Shalt Not Kill"
but a Minority seems not to heed
so I need to know what else we can do

when police face someone with black skin
and pull their triggers
until their guns are empty.

Dear President Bush,

I had a few thoughts regarding your press conference
on August 21, 2006.

We have a one-year anniversary coming.
and I respectfully request you do not send flowers.
They cannot mask the odor of new shoe leather
from Condi's New York shopping spree,
the reek of ebony/alabaster bodies left to rot,
a girl dreaming of the urine she slept in when
thousands were shoved into a space too small to contain
their griefs, worries, and waste.

Those levees, as flimsy as your excuses.
Due to this government's willful neglect,
at least 1,836 people were killed,
$81.2 billion of property damage,
and a new American diaspora was created
when children were separated from their families
and flung across 49 states.

In lieu of flowers,
tell your mother to apologize
for believing that being warehoused
in the Houston Astrodome
is the equivalent of hospitality.

Give Louisiana its share of the oil and gas revenues.
Demand that Allstate pay its insurance claims
and if you lack
the political will
to do so
send your letter of resignation.

Footnotes

March 2, 1955
she was kicked
textbooks knocked away
dragged off by her arms
and arrested at 15
for not giving up her seat
on a Montgomery bus.
She cried out
I done paid my dime. I got my rights.

First to plead not guilty
for violating the bus ordinance
yet
most do not know her name because
Claudette Colvin
became
an unwed mother.

October 21, 1955
Mary Louise Smith
was 18
she refused to surrender her seat
and
she too was passed
over
false rumors
that her father was a drunk.

Rosa Parks, with her light skin
and stable middle-aged
married life became the
cause celebre.

These brave black girls,
plaintiffs in *Browder v. Gayle,*
the case that desegregated the buses,
are footnotes,.
because
under America's microscope
our heroes must be as angels.

Spleen and Sawdust

What was once a mighty oak
standing tall in Louisiana
is now a stump

no oak wilt
no insects
no caterpillars
no lightning bolt

but for
a question,
black and gold nooses
sit-ins
a threat with a pen
a fire
fisticuffs
a shotgun
taunting
a middle finger
a beating…

…they cut the tree down.

What will they do for the people?

For Viola Liuzzo
A Dada

1965 inspired march on Selma
television reports Alabama authorities
official billy clubs
thrashed civil rights
skulls
the elderly.

Angered by Dr. King's
sympathetic religious telegrams
40-year-old
Viola Liuzzo
white Michigan housewife
mother
left her husband against who
chased
shot twice in the head and civil
Alabama state court
they were on their way back to KKK
these local whites violate
Alabama first
Three men found not guilty. "Let's get them!"

First degree murder
be damned
brutal response
guilty of conspiring
sentenced to ten years each
federal prison

Premonition
signaled
somebody is going to get killed.
100 mph
traffic light

Look baby brother.
Murderers responded.

Something is going to happen today.

She was driving civil rights
two shots escaped
On March 25
Stopped at a
Traffic light

Pulled up next to them,
two shots escaped, she
dead against the wheel
Leroy Moton
tried to rouse her
culprits came back
playing dead in her blood
a light in the car
Leroy Moton escaped
playing dead
escaped darkened swamps
relayed the story

Montgomery passed out cold

J. Edgar Hoover had
hit the brakes
crazy
against Liuzzo
he turned off the lights
painted her
a smear campaign.
She was dead.
Unstable woman,
civil rights was her only concern.

Alabama mourn,
her husband Anthony
five children
Penny 18
Mary 17
Thomas 13
Anthony Jr. 10
Sally 6.
Children,
every American is responsible
And
I feel it.
Workers,
stir up
civil rights.
Justice in trouble!
Don't die in vain.

Shelwanda Riley

Who let her out at 1 a.m.
to be stopped and frisked?

When she kicked
and screamed
and twisted
her tiny 15-year-old frame
and bit that cop
she was punched in the face
pepper sprayed
and is well on her way
to becoming
one of the million
of us
locked up.

Beauty and Movement

Unbelieving, I
scratched my diamond ring against
my mirror. My brothers'
blood streaked across
my ebony reflection.

I ran to my car.
My tank was full. I went for
a long drive to clear my head,

and in southern Nigeria
gas flares burn.
Greasy executives slide around
questions and responsibility.
A tribal chief pockets the cash
and stuffs his living room with a leather sofa.

Ken Saro-Wiwa, executed.

A man in a suit coughs from the
slaughterhouse smoke and peeks inside
the rusting tin shacks.
He checks OK on the form.
His boss will smile as he stamps on the official seal.

Children wander, wonder, founder.
Hope shrugs its shoulders.

A native engineer applies to be a company man.
He is offered a mop.

Young men join gangs and kidnap foreign workers.
Ransom is paid. Oil resumes its flow then leaks.
It does not mix with water.

A fisherman casts his net and waits.
When Heaven
drops its black blanket across
the sky, he walks home with
nothing to cook.

A Sonnet

Millions of ebony eyes have cried,
Across unforgiving sands they have toiled.
A boy is now mute, he watched his father die
in this genocidal, other war, (for oil)?

Ranks in the refugee camps have swelled
Monsters are castrating Sudanese sons,
A mother's daughter drowned in a well.
The girl's kept dress, now the color of dun.

Rapes, burned villages, rotting corpses, vile,
Hints of sanctions; in the face of such dearth?
Al-Bashir stands by his public denial.
What is the life of a Sudanese worth?

Why must the innocent sing that old song?
Oh Lord, how many? How much? For how long?

Yon Desod
(for Reverend Joseph Dantica)

Bury our friends or die, they said,
his 81-year-old body under a neighbor's bed.
Three days
gangs plundered his home and church
burned his 50-year-old school.

He surrendered to his family's 30-year-old plea.
Emigrate to the States!

Off the plane in Miami,
they asked how long he'd stay.
He said.
"I will be killed if I go back to Port-au-Prince."
He and his son, arrested.
At Krome,
they looked him over, saw no
cherubic face and elfin grin.

His prostate and
blood pressure medicine, taken away.

The day before he died
he collapsed
a medic sidestepped the vomit
and announced,
he's faking.

Somebody, clean this up

The Human Knot

The year that Tupac died, I
seeking change, assumed
the role of teacher would be a simple task
degree from N.Y.U
took a job in the South Bronx
where I would have grown up

To teach my people
descendants of Africa
Tainos
Arawaks
Aztecs

I thought I had nothing to fear.
One day six boys came into my room.
One said, "you know, we could rape you right here".

People of color made occasional appearances
in our textbooks, overflowing with weary knowledge.
Tried to fill in the gaps with J.A. Rogers,
Ivan Van Sertima, Howard Zinn, simplified.

Delivered lessons on Incas, Aztecs, Tainos.
Bartholomew de las Casas.
Some wrote consciously and copiously.
Others merely copied.
Tuned in, tuned out, talked back, walked out.

Kids played games with my name--
Mango-coco-cherry.
Like the sweet icies sold by street corner vendors
on hot sticky days.

I struggled to understand their limited retention.
Bad behavior, frequent detention.
Refrains of "boring" assaulted in my ears.
End of school days often found me in tears.

Maritza yelled at me for calling her house.
Miguel said I wasn't a real teacher.
Pedro told me to go back to Africa.
Darryl got in my face with a flurry of fuck yous.

Chanel rolled her eyes.
Asia snarled, "what" every time I said her name.
Chris threw my childhood books all over the room.
Jon said what I had to say wasn't important.

How could I break through concrete walls of will
With my consciousness nursed on the lyrical silk
Of Public Enemy and X-Clan's "Verbal Milk"
as opposed to the violent vent
from the Similac of 50 Cent?

People told me I was soft
So, I swallowed some urban grit.
In lieu of poetic verses,
I spit threatening curses

thinking fear would earn me respect.
Yet I thought of my son in school.
Soon realized that was not
the example I wanted to set.

Angry at all those brown and black faces,
teaching wasn't what I thought it would be.
Yet giving up was contrary
to the activist in me.

Frederick Douglass said without struggle,
there is no progress.
I vowed to work so
"them" and "those" would be "us" and "we".

So, with NYU degree,
in the South Bronx
where I would have grown up
to teach my people
descendants of Africa
Tainos
Arawaks
Aztecs
I reopened my heart

sang songs
read Tupac's poems aloud,
played music,
showed movies
and for Hispanic Heritage Month
Rosanna brought pastellitos.
I pretended not to taste the beef--
that I don't eat--
as I bit into the flaky crust.

If New York Could Talk

Come admire the museums adorned with artwork.
Come see the Mets and Yankees play.
Come make big bucks on Wall Street
If you want to afford to stay.

I have so much to offer,
artists, writers, and tourists too.
Play in my parks, shop on Fifth Avenue.
Visit the Brooklyn Zoo.

Come tour the churches of Harlem.
Savor the world's cuisines.
Gaze up at my towering skyscrapers,
Take in the Broadway scene.

Sway to the pulse of my music
Jazz, blues, and doo-wop
Salsa, meringue, bachata
R&B and, of course, hip-hop.

Be forewarned, of my hard truths—
Underneath the beat of sauntering feet
Lay unmarked graves,
Of many slaves,
Beneath my gold-paved streets.

They razed Seneca Village,
Evicted its residents, the times, so dark
To make room for the grandeur
Of today's Central Park.

And as you stroll along Columbus Circle
You'd better watch your step.
You might want to avoid the homeless,
the crazy and unkempt.

Drugs, gangs, and brutal cops
All have taken their toll
on my vulnerable people.
Their griefs sully my soul.

You can't *all* be successful,
Of this, there is no doubt.
If you have no safety net,
I'll chew you up and spit you out.

The Rush

I was eight
and on a class trip
to visit the Statue of Liberty

There were marching dozens in front
and dozens tightly behind
wending our way up
the narrow prison-grey staircase
passing seats, with me
wondering which ladies
and gentlemen of leisure sat there
fanning themselves
up the 354 steps.

Claustrophobia setting in
and my stomach twisted in a giant knot,
I wanted to turn backwards and run
towards space and fresh air,
but I couldn't wait to
tower over the New York skyline
and gaze across at the World Trade Center.

When I finally made my grand entrance into the crown
I was only able to glimpse the bright light
of the midday sun,
a patch of blue
from the Hudson River,
and endless sky,
before we pushed toward our rapid descent.

I never went back.

Then there was 9/11.

If I can ever retrace my steps
into that windowed space
I will plant my feet,
rest my head in the cup of my hands,
and eat Time.

Utopia

I know it is naïve
to conceive of a world
where there is
work
fresh water
free speech
for everyone
fruit and cereal on
each child's morning breath as they
walk to school
and each dis-ease
has a cure.

I can dream.

Untitled

Atop a cliff along the Atlantic coast
We African ghosts of America
wander and cry out,
What is my name?

III

Nom

I got this quote from Stokely Carmichael secondhand from
my college professor, so forgive me if it isn't right:
If you put a kitten in an oven, when you take it out, is it a muffin?
If you put Africans in America, aren't they still Africans?

Impressionable, and immediately impressed
deeply immersed in my socio-political historical linguistic identity,
I considered changing my birth name.

Combed through three books of African names
with the care I give to my hair.
I found the perfect antithesis of my self-image:
Jamilah, beautiful
Amirh, princess
Nkenge, of superior mind.

I was old enough not to need my parents' permission, but
when presented with my new moniker,
Mommy's lukewarm "that's nice"
led me to recall my birth name's story.

As I grew in her womb, she too, had run through a book of names
and settled on Kendra.
Daddy didn't like it, or the dozens of others
but he loved a Carla Thomas song
"Gee Whiz"
and the name Michele.

Daddy's pride in his southern-rooted surname
made me pause--
my great-great grandparents
planted peanuts and cotton in the blazing
North Carolina sun
and beget seventeen children,
one named John, who had a son Boston
who had a son, Melvin, my father.

I placed the name book back in the closet.
When I held my newborn son in my arms,
I found a kingly name from West Africa
and whispered it in his ear.

Grandma, Donna, and Me

For Grandma Ballew

No statues erected in your honor.
No great works of art adorned with your face.
No novels tell your story.
But the world was quite blessed by your grace.

Neither racism, hardship, nor grief
could your courage and faith ever shatter.
You inspired us to face the trials of life
with the weapons of love and laughter.

You, with five children in tow,
left the South and your unhappy home.
It must have been your faith that God
would never leave you alone.

Poverty never stripped you of your pride.
You raised your children to have high self-esteem:
"As long as your hair and shoes are clean and neat,
it doesn't matter what you have on in between."

You watched your sons strive to achieve,
And saw three of them to the grave,
Your graceful strength, even when stricken with cancer,
Taught me how a Christian soldier should behave.

I'll never have to search my history books
to celebrate an African queen--
I'll summon your image from precious memories
And speak your name, Pauline.

For Aunt Marguerite

I juxtaposed our photographs today
To see what I could see
You were twenty-one
And I was twenty-three.

The violence of racism
Never invaded my own life
Your perseverance inspires me.
You rose above the strife.

You always sought out leadership
And decided to teach
For the same reason that I did,
So many young souls to reach.

So many hardships came your way.
You were taken off your track.
But as my elders always remind me
You had a hearty laugh.

Auntie, the you that I remember,
Would open her smooth-skinned arms
And say, "Carla Michele, come give me a kiss!"
Then in your Southern charm,
You promised us children trips to India,
Or some exotic isle.
Our parents grinned and shook their hands,
And we'd politely smile.

Sometimes I forgot all you'd been through
In your difficult life's station,
I should have given you more credit
For your gift of imagination.

I wish I had the presence of mind
All those times that I was there,
To say, "Auntie, tell all that you remember,"
And I had stayed a while longer
In that pink lounge chair.

I'd listen to your stories of Grandma Florence
And her sisters too.
I can't remember all their names
But you and Grandma do.
If you can hear me as I recite this poem.
Please do one thing before you go
Tell our loved ones up there with you
That we miss all of you so.

If I could travel back in time
Just so that I could be
Young when all of you were young
And see what you did see.

Then I could say I really knew the Auntie I remember
But on this life lesson you can bet
As I remember all I've learned
Our progeny won't forget.

Black Pearl
(For Saundra McPherson)

When I watch "the Wiz"
'cause I love to watch her dance

I keep rewinding the tape
to freeze the moment when the camera captures her beaming face
Almond eyes wide with delight
Radiant smile
Arms outstretched towards the stars
Reveling her moment of glory

When I see it
I still think
What I first thought
As a young girl

I want to be like that

Self-possessed
Alluring
Beautiful
Comfortable in her golden-brown skin
Graceful poetry in rhythmic motion

When I was a child
She enchanted me—
This free spirit
So unlike my timid self

She was walks through Greenwich Village
And Washington Square Park
Dips in the fountain during the summer
Magic shows
Late night jam sessions on the conga and tambourines
Disturbing the neighbors and not caring
Picnics and funny stories

I loved her embrace of Blackness
Naturally

Afro to braids
To locs
To braids
To Afro
To braids
To Afro
She taught Mommy to cornrow our hair and we loved it

I was mesmerized by her dance career
"Oh yes," she said, "I performed with Billy Dee"
"Ask him, he'd remember me,"
and danced with Godfrey Cambridge
performed with Duke Ellington's band.
She was Miss Green for Ntozake.
Yeah, Saundra
a wonder to behold
a colored girl
who never had enough of life
she ran to the end of the rainbow
chasing dreams
searching for a pot of gold
never attaining material wealth

but she was rich:
abundant talent
passion
love
and hard-earned wisdom.

She was fierce

Dancer
Teacher
Nurturing mother/father
To Eric
Kiameshia
She gave them her all
And then some—
Sustaining love
Black pride
Book knowledge
Knowledge of self
Lessons on karate to dance to music

They are
A testament to her spirit
Brilliant
Compassionate
Knowing
Saundra is in the village of the ancestors
But she's still here.
She's my muse when I write
I hear her in Eric's music
And feel her in Kiameshia's zest for life
She's all over Nasif's face
And in Nailah's eyes.

Donna, Daddy, and Me

Daddy

Somebody should have told the hospital about Feng Shui--
having the foot of your bed facing the door
is an invitation to Death.

Daddy's feet were the first things I saw.

Daddy was
Larger than life
A gentle giant tossing me up in the air when I was a baby
Giving Mommy fits
But I laughed
'cuz even then I knew
he'd never drop me.

My protector.
With my small hands encircled by his, I was safe.

Those hands steadied me as I learned to ride my bike—
the red one he bought me for my fifth birthday.

Daddy, who saved my life when I was four
I had jumped into the pool
without looking and was drowning.

Daddy was
heavy footsteps
the opening and shutting of drawers
and the front door
as he made his way to work, almost every day.

Daddy was
the mustache that tickled my face when he kissed my cheek
the scent of gasoline and Lifebuoy soap and that Magic shaving cream
I hated because it smelled like old clay,
but loved because it meant
he was home.

Daddy was our buddy.
We'd call,
"Daddy, we have a surprise for you".
Us, giggling with anticipation
he, feigning surprise
when we smacked him with our pillows
laughing, as he tossed us on our beds
straddling his back as we played horsie.
Giddyup
Joyfully, we walked barefoot across his back.

Daddy was
pancakes on Sunday,
echoes of Aretha's *Amazing Grace* blasting
Wholly Holy

Daddy was
long car trips set to music.
Singing Moody's Blues in the car
There I go
There I go
There I go
There I gooooooooooooo--
We laughed as his deep voice cracked.

Daddy was Harlem
Piano and flute at Harlem School of the Arts
Better Pie Crust cinnamon buns and sticky fingers
Dinners at Copeland's and 22 West
Collard greens, yams, macaroni and cheese, and fried chicken
Sundays at Abyssinian.

Daddy was wisdom:
Know thyself
Sit down and watch *Like It Is*
You are because we are, therefore, you will be.
Third World became First World.
Ivan Van Sertima
Cheik Anta Diop
Dr. Leonard Jeffries
Professor Scobie

Saturdays reading to Ms. Mulzac at her Liberation Bookstore
where black was beautiful, and so was I.
Nikki Giovanni's *Ego Tripping*
Toni Morrison's *Bluest Eye*
Alice Childress' *A Short Walk*

Daddy was culture.
Noel Pointer's poignant violin.
Sweet Honey and the Rock.
Do Lord Remember Me.
The Piano Lesson.
Mama, I Want to Sing.

Daddy was a forward thinker,
Pointing Donna and I towards the horizon of opportunity.
He pulled our arms from around his legs, and said, go.
Home would be a refuge but not a resting place.

So we went, making progress, getting degrees, making mistakes.
Through it all
Daddy was advisor
cheerleader
admirer.

He told me I was his hero.

And then, as cancer shattered bones,
he walked like he was treading shards of glass.
I soaked up stories
committed the rhythm of his breath and
his butter soft skin to memory
brushed his hair
held his hands
stroked the crooked fingernail on his right hand
that had been ripped out by a machine at work.

When Daddy was gone
I screamed
I cried
and
although I know Daddy is all around and through me—
his books
music
ambitions--
before they took him
I eased his yellow wristband
LIVE STRONG
from his arm
and wrapped it around mine.

Potpourri

Fulton Terrace--
East 169th Street between Fulton and Third Avenues—
sits on a hill.

Directly across the narrow street was a church
and a lot made vacant when the apartment building
that sat on it burned down the day I was born.

Nana and Pop-Pop lived in apartment 18B

Pop-Pop stretched our names like rubber bands
"Www---elll, if it isn't Do—nna and Car—la".

Nana's emphatic laughter still echoes in my ear.
Ha!

The beige plastic-covered sofa stuck to my thighs in the summers.
The upright chair was the color of sky before a rainstorm.
Glass candy dishes offered lemon, lime, cherry candies
that I rolled around my mouth until they were soft enough to chew.

In one of my favorite photographs
Pop-Pop sits in his olive-green recliner
holding me as a newborn.

The terrace was my fortress.
I saw clear across the Bronx, and from there
one sunny-rainy day,
I saw my first rainbow.

I can still smell Nana's macaroni and cheese,
edges slightly and perfectly browned.
Stuffed peppers brimmed with rice and meat.
Buttery crescent rolls covered and kept warm with a dishcloth.

Nana's jewelry box was like an oyster.
We'd pry it open,
then don the silver and pearl necklaces
that hung low on my sister and me.

Mrs. Boddie lived next door.
Her dog's yelping puppies
squirmed in my five-year old hands.

One Christmas, surrounded by boxes of brand-new clothes,
Nana's doll with an old-fashioned ivory dress
dried my tears when I got no toys.

"Happy 55th Anniversary" in careful cursive writing
on a delectable vanilla cake.
I watched their delicate kiss.

When old age ushered in sickness,
Nana was in a hospital bed.
Diabetes robbed her of several toes.
I leaned against Daddy's six-foot-two-inch frame and sobbed.
"Hi, Nana" we said.
Through morphine-induced stupor
her blue-grey eyes looked through us,
then she turned her head.

Pop-Pop's dementia rendered
independence a newly slippery thing.
Rage overpowered love, and he
threw a chair at Daddy on the last visit.
"Yes, I brought you this food myself," I lied.
Daddy sat and waited in the car.

The refrigerator became a haven for baby roaches.
Sadness and loneliness lingered like a bad smell.

For Aunt Joan

When I'm missing them
I envision the living room on St. Nicholas Ave.
Sam Cooke is playing.
Aunt Joan is teaching Daddy to dance--
1 2 cha cha cha 3 4 cha cha cha.

Daddy's little sister,
auburn hair stylishly short,
fingers and toenails painted various shades of red,
deep-set eyes, dimpled smile,
laughter a soprano hum,
whose buxom curves demanded
an unhurried walk.

When I was one, she held my hands
as I walked across Nana's and Pop-Pop's couch.

She gave us golden angels inscribed with our names.
We wiggled them to hear the bells tinkle as we hung
them on our Christmas tree.
We got sweaters embroidered with our initials and a cherry--
I had yellow, Donna red.
Another year, a Barbie trailer.

We crawled on the floor with our cousin John-John
and cried for weeks when his daddy took him away.

When she brought Greg home,
he was handsome and brown and laughing.
I fell in love with love at their wedding.

Birthday cards every year,
a jar of Let's Jam so I could style my hair,
and her proud presence at my college graduation.
To my relief she had no wintry words
for the life growing in me.

Days after I gave birth
as I lay across the couch holding Khari
she called to announce her cancer.

What is this envy of beauty?

She came to visit
her hair only black roots
still stunning, she
took off her wig.
I figured you all wouldn't mind--
like we would love her less.

Months later, we had a picnic
John-John was back, and grown.
So was her hair.

We took pictures and ate and laughed.
I sent them to the studio, but
only received an apology.

A year later the doctor called Daddy to say
if you want to say goodbye you better come now.
We rushed to her bedside.

I stroked the rising moons in
her perfect unpolished fingernails.

Aunt Joan's face alight with love
she did not speak.
The nurse brought a paper cup to her adverse lips--
oh, exquisite enmity.

At her funeral
she was in a pink taffeta dress
awful brown wig and a layer of brown powder
that was not her color
the organ singer forgot the words to His Eye Is On the Sparrow.

John-John took off his necklace and laid it at her side.
Daddy's voice cracked as he said his goodbye.
Uncle Greg slouched in his chair by her casket,
the first man I ever saw cry up close.

I wore her earrings for a few months--
14 carat gold hoops fringed with teal and maroon.
One of them dropped on the street.
For ten minutes I searched.
I gave up because I was running late for work.
I kept the spare.
Someday a jeweler will make another
with an iron-willed clutch.

Last Request

As I stood at your bedside
I didn't focus on how thin you've gotten
or the few months you have left.
I thought about how much you look like Grandma,
with her walnut complexion
cheekbones
same dorsum of the nose,
smile, like a quarter crescent moon,
her, reed thin and 18,
birthing you at home,
her biggest baby, at nine pounds,
hot towels around her waist to steam you out.
I tried to picture you sitting on her lap,
her slathering your hands with molasses and handing you a feather
to keep you laughing and busy
through her cooking and cleaning.
Sorry it took us a couple of minutes
to find 1 Kings so we could read along
and that we didn't know the story of Elijah,
but we understand its point, your point, that
you have accepted God's will.

But before you are taken up to heaven
in the chariot of fire,
I am hoping you will let me, us, in.
Share some more stories of your Kentucky childhood
the bigness/smallness/warmth/draftiness of the houses you all lived in,
how much you teased Mommy or protected her from the pranks of
my three other uncles,
Grandfather's sober moments,
if he gave hugs or sage advice,
before Grandma wearied of the drinking, gambling, constant evictions,
left for New York to make a fatherless home for six,
what it was like
to be man of the house at the age of 12,
your studies at Cooper Union,
your time in the Army,
why you choose lifelong bachelorhood and gave your life over to the Lord.
I hope there are a few of your drawings left to salvage
from your shopping cart.
I promise, we will find it soon.
In the meantime, please, let us in.

African Beauties

What beautiful flowers.
Are they from a wedding?

My uncle's funeral.
I am so sorry.

Her eldest daughter leaned in to smell my calla lilies.
Don't touch them, her mother warned, as she shifted the baby on her hip.
You don't have to get close. You can still smell them from where you are.

I held them forward.
The little girl stood on her tiptoes in her white patent leather shoes,
shut her raven eyes, and deeply inhaled two times.

Her mother and I wished each other well.
When I got off the elevator, the daughter called out: *Bye!*

As soon as I got home, I poured water in my vase, eased the flowers inside,
and placed it on my dining table.

I got a copper penny from my change jar and dropped it in the water.
My mother always does that.

The lean of green unopened bulbs, the sprawl of white petals,
the fragrance unfolding through my kitchen, made me smile.

Thought about that girl, her flawless brown skin against white satin and
orange lace.
She will likely grow up in this city, where she will learn to

stand firm as she waits to squeeze into rumbling trains
that come to whistling, screeching slow halts,
watch for wandering, unwelcome hands,
and sleep through the wail of sirens.

I should have given her a flower from my bouquet.
Her mother seemed like the type to teach her how make a keepsake.

Spring

Walking through tufts
of green grass, I sidestep newly sprouting violets.

Next to a bed of peach and butter-colored tulips, I see
a dandelion weed in full bloom. Remembering

happier childhood days, I pluck it. I close my eyes, and
blow wisps of white into the air. As the spores float,

seeking their new homes, I whisper my wish
to hear my father's voice.

Bits and Pieces

When I was a child, I waged bloodless wars
over the radio. Strictly a fan of pop and hip-hop,
I imitated what I thought was whining—
didn't know drat about scat—
when Daddy played jazz.
I wasn't diggin' it
until I heard my cousin Eric
play the drums.

A dig a dig a dig a diga dat.
Rat a-tat-a-tat.
Damn, he was a cool cat.
The brush of his blades
like a lover licking skin.

Then he burst forth
with kinetic/frenetic/foot pounding
flawless flow of polyrhythmic staccato.

My feet tapping/fingers involuntarily/snapping

A Japanese man jerked his neck in fits
that somehow kept time

my sister and I poked fun
yet I understood.

As a student
of Black history,
I turned to
Leroi Jones

his *Blues People*
only
unraveled bits and pieces
of the mystery
'cause how can you sum up a music derived
from drums denied,
a capella cries,
field hollers,
backs bent picking cotton,
spirituals sung whisper-quiet,
Congo Square calabashes,
drums and singing,
before the masters come.
Le jass.

Emancipation Proclamation
Freedom and travelin' shoes.
Personal space
to play the banjo
sing the blues about
the trials and tribulations of the individual

brass instruments
Napoleonic marching bands
Clarinets/Tubas/Trombones/Trumpets
Negro nuances
Call and response.
Improvised singing in the breaks.
Marching to funeral dirges set to 4/4 time.
Celebration of passed lives
2/4 quadrilles and minuets.

Grunts and moans
black men wielding hammers
slamming steel in time.

As he hauled coal in New Orleans
Louis Armstrong stood outside Pete Lala's
listening as Joe Oliver blew
that wah wah
with a plunger or hat
in the bell of his horn.

Jelly Roll Morton's piano
made the trickin' go down easy.

Le jass / dirty music.

White show music plus black rhythm
Ragtime
Harmonic and melodic complexities

1917 they turned off
the red lights in Storyville
trains, cars, feet head North
to the beat of
the quarter-tone pitch.

Mamie Smith's It's Right Here For You
Ma Rainey's black bottom puttin' em in a trance
Bessie Smith's Downhearted Blues.
Race music on record.

The New Negro.
Jimmie Lunceford
Coleman Hawkins' big band jazz.
Call and response.
Cab Calloway.
Hi-de-de-hi-di-ho.
Duke Ellington and Billy Strayhorn.
Take The A Train, to
Sugar Hill.

Fletcher Henderson and Don Redman
swinging in Roseland,
couples doing the Lindy hop
to Count Basie's Jumpin' at the Woodside.

At the Savoy
Big Bea carried Shorty George off the floor on her back,
not to be outdone

Frankie threw Freda, and the aerial was born
but
when swing was sameness and soullessness
beboppers
brought back the blues
with the bass
contrast, conflict,
cymbal riffs, and
solo replies.

Monday nights at Minton's
Roy Eldridge dueling Dizzy Gillespie
Ben Webster taking on Lester Young
and young cats with horns in hand
awaiting a beckon, then a smile.

I took note of my generation's
call and response

Somebody say oh yeah
Oh yeah!

Squeezed by urban living,
Grandmaster Flash and the Furious Five
created "The Message".
Hip hop sat on the knees of bebop and cool
and gave birth to
Gangstarr's *Jazzamatazz,*
A Tribe Called Quest's *Low End Theory,*

and Mos Def's "Umi Says".

One night I
stole out for a walk
and heard music
in the call of the whippoorwill

When I drive
Miles, Monk, Ella, Sarah,
Billie, Dinah, Coltrane
slacken my tightened neck
and lull me from beta to alpha
state
I tap my thumb against the wheel
to keep time
always wishing
I could make
that silly child I was
apologize to Daddy
and the ancestors.

I'd rebuke her gently,
'cause I know she didn't know.

Coal, squeezed by pressure, is a diamond.

IV

Elusive I

i have spent half my life
figuring out why
i always liked looking in windows
more than mirrors

The Human Manifesto

I am a
Double-standard.

I demand honesty,
Yet I lie.

Love is the zenith of human emotion,
Still I hate.

Materialism evokes the negative side of human nature,
But I want.

Serenity nurtures the soul,
Nevertheless, I anger.

Bravery is the exultation of the spirit.
Alas, cowardice is anchored in my heart.

I advocate the highest morals for mankind,

I
 Can't
  Comply.

Honesty

The morning of my baptism
I shut myself in my room
I fell to my knees
asking You to enter my heart
and a rush of electric waves coursed through me.
That morning, in shrouds of white, I was dipped in the
Baptism pool as the choir sang above.

Yet
dozens of Sundays have passed,
some on record in my journal
with church programs and sermon notes,
but most
find me doing housework
or
weary from mangled worldly demands,
fast asleep.

I know that a clean house and clean clothes
do less
than a pure mind and heart
to give me rest
so
I pray that You will be patient with me
as I move beyond
mouthing the words
to Psalm 23,
singing, clapping
tapping my feet
along with my favorite hymns,
and my annual vow to go to church
every week.

Please guide
my thoughts
my speech
my pen
my feet
as I make
these baby steps
towards You.

Testimony

To
discover
the
Divine
I
within
is
greater
than
all
the
world.

Work in Progress

In the quiet of the empty campus square
we sat chest to back.

Enveloped in the smell of musk,
squeezing secret throbbings,
weighing the yeses against the no's,
I gently leaned into his kiss. My tears
salty like Friday night fried fish.

I closed my eyes, as the breeze
caressed our skin.

Back at the dorm
I met your accusing eyes.

What about John?

In The Light
(Inspired by P.N. and R.W.)

I.
Aged sixteen, she was
waiting in a clinic, alone
surrounded by other girls and women
wondering about their whys.

She lay flat on her back,
knees, propped
the doctor rammed her fist
into the room of her womb.

You feel like fourteen weeks,
she growled.

Her warm belly shuddered against
the cold ultrasound probe.
It revealed the fetus to be eleven weeks.
She said,
we can proceed.

Lying flat on her back
counting backwards from one hundred
breathing deeply,
consciousness lapsing into dreams
of strawberry fields.

She awakened to white light
tingly and shivering
head spun by rotating walls.

The floor dodged her feet.

Blood seeped through her gown.
She wanted to get up and go,
but the weight of the world
was sitting on her head.

Sipping tea,
Clarity returned.

She dressed and headed out to the street, elated by
her newfound freedom from fear.

She was
once again, college-bound.

II.
She watched as Nora bravely held her fatherless baby
in front of the congregation.
Pastor said,
"You know we don't approve".
Even still, he reminded her
she could lean on the church
as she fulfilled her motherly duties.

Recounting Nora's past pregnancy scares
she sat there, smugly superior.
Only God knew her secret shame,
and He wasn't telling.

III.
And when she was
amidst school chatter and laughter
the tears came
for the boy/girl, and
she ran into
the vomit green bathroom.

Confession

One day one of my girls cried in my arms
a man had pulled her off the street
got her pregnant
she had to have an abortion at 13

A man had pulled her off the street
I got her some information about counseling
She had to have an abortion at 13
The next year there was another girl

who kept her head down on her desk
there were whispers she had been raped
one boy teased her about it in class
I reamed into him, made him apologize

there were whispers she had been raped
couldn't fathom how her rape was funny
I reamed into him, made him apologize
I wondered if he ever really was sorry

The next year after class
as I was gathering papers and chalk
another girl revealed
she was in counseling because she was raped

as I was gathering papers and chalk
I asked if we could talk later
She was in counseling because she was raped
I was relieved because

we never discussed it again.
I didn't want to pry.
Was she afraid of another brush-off?
I will never know.

I didn't want to pry.
The next year there was another girl
who passed me her journal, a page and a half
about her molestation.

Another girl
looking to me for more.
I fumbled.
Another girl.
"Are you in counseling," I asked.
I fumbled.
"Sweetie, this is too heavy. I don't know how to help you."

I passed the notebook back.
She never showed it to me again.
Why didn't I just give her a hug?
Compliment her on her strength?

She never showed it to me again.
Why didn't I just give her a hug?
Compliment her on her strength?
I just passed the notebook back.

A Sestina

The random train station graffiti, an offense.
I held my breath so I wouldn't surrender
to the stench of urine. Having Derek hold me was key to my identity.
My adolescent insecurity would be released
in his arms, so I would wait. Never thought I might be raped
by some random guilty party.

Seventeen years old. Too shy to be the life of any party.
Being in a desolate place, my only offense.
A man asked me for a token, and since I saw no hint of rape,
I said no with a smile. His sudden knife demanded silent surrender.
My God, what if I were not released?
If I were, could I repair my identity?

I cursed myself for this risk to my identity.
Would Derek also be considered a guilty party?
I prayed to God to secure my release.
He searched for money in my jeans. His roaming hands, an offense
"Wait," he hissed. "I want to make it with you." That fucking knife. Surrender.
My innocence shattered by rape?

Rape,
by a brotha. He cared nothing of my pro-black identity.
He backed me against the wall, I pinned my dreams on surrender
and some compassion from the guilty party.
I had always found supplication an offense,
yet I begged to be released.

Hope was renewed that I could be released,
when he told me to walk up the stairs. Likely towards a private rape.
This monster snarled as he asked my name. What an offense.
I refused to answer, to maintain the sanctity of my identity.
As I inched up the steps, the guilty party,
allowed his eyes to roam my adolescent body. Rage against this offense
crushed the idea of surrender.

Fear was surrendered.
I pumped my long legs toward release.
From the twisted mouth and violent dick of this guilty party,
this monster, who considered rape.
I could forge my adult identity.
I rejoiced over his foiled offense.

I never reported the attempted rape; after all, I had been released.
I feared in surrendering details, the police would identify me as a guilty party.
I was merely happy my attacker failed to commit his intended offense.

Dear Sir,

You leered at me
and called me out of my name.

What is it
about my presence
that unnerves you?
I stride down these streets
as a proud black woman who
dares to dream
should.

I keep my eyes fixed on
Righteousness.

I hold myself in too high a regard
to acquiesce to disrespect.

I am not a whore.

Does it anger you
that I aspire to something more?

I smile at a world
that conspires to destroy me
but I hear you berate me under your breath

Are you not
black like me?

Why don't you give me praise instead of hatred?

Is it my audacity
to be
or your lack of courage
to do so

BIORHYTHM

When I'm in class with them
I listen to the drumbeats
focus on the steps
and adjust to the vibrations.
I keep trying and trying
until I've got it down
and I start groovin'
but then
Torkwase calls me out.
I feel all eyes on me
(even though no one's really paying attention)
and I can't do the steps
or keep the time
my svelte dancer's body, awkward and slow.

I rush home with tearing eyes,
slamming the door when I arrive.

Now I'm all alone
and can be my secret self.

Behind closed doors
I'm a lithe Bambara girl
arching my back
jutting out my breasts
swinging my head, arms, and legs without restraint.

The other women there
shout for joy
run up, slap the ground at my fast-flying feet
shouting, Asante
(thank you, girl, for being you)
the men
stare at me in wonder
(how must she be in the act of love)
and they drum faster
to arouse me into a greater frenzy.
I show them how good I really am

                Damn

If I could do that when I'm NOT alone
If I could let the world see that I am a bonafide sister
who loves herself
and really can get down
instead of an out-of-shape, out-of-touch Black woman
who dances like she's on her last leg.

Simplicity

the best lesson
I ever learned
about life was
to spit out
watermelon seeds
and to suck
all the meat
off the bone

Cacoethes

I turned 35 today.
I arose from my bed, happily
sent my son over to my mother.

I soaked in the tub
marveled over my still-soft skin
toweled myself dry
caressed my skin with cocoa butter
sprayed perfume on my wrists, behind my ears, and knees
painted my toenails with mauve polish
and slipped on
my brand new
black
strappy
high heeled
Aldo sandals
that accentuate the curve of my calves.

As I clicked my heels against concrete streets
I realized
they sure do hurt my black woman's feet
size 10
toes long like a piano player's fingers
just like my Nana's.

As I tiptoed across Manhattan
with my amused best friend in her soft-soled shoes
I cursed every shoe designer
who only sees beauty in reed-thin women with diminutive feet.

When I got home I flung my tormentors off,
concluding that I should throw them away
in favor of flat soft-soled shoes
but
curves are seductive--
girls anticipate their budding breasts
men obsess over Jennifer's and Beyonce's derrieres
wolves bay at the voluptuous moon
and the world rejoiced to learn the Earth was round.

And considering my comeliness
in my brand new strappy black Aldo sandals
I tucked them back into my closet
for the next special occasion.

Pulchritude

I got to know my mother well,
straddled between her thighs
as she gently combed
oiled
brushed
braided
twisted
my thick kinky hair
tenderly.
We spoke of love,
family history,
death.
Sometimes we were silent,
the only sound being the joyful noise
Black hair often makes.

As I grew older
long, straight hair captured my fascination.
I too, wanted the adoration.

I endured the burning stench of the hot comb
searing through my precious locks.

Oh, the outrageous things we do to our hair
with tension, heat, and chemicals.

I thought it was pretty
but it was only unnatural--
Humidity and hot showers humbled
my op-pressed hair, as
my carefully crafted curls shrank into spiraling coils.

And then there was Diana's
glorious, straightened mane
that kissed her shoulders and
weathered all kinds of weather.

Envisioning myself with Diana's lustrous beauty,
I found myself in her mother's kitchen
eyes tearing,
gripping the chair—
I thought I was there for a relaxer--
scalp afire,
awaiting
the initiation of my virgin hair.
In lieu of an alluring coiffure
I went home with scars and three inches less hair.

As the scabs crusted over and fell off
and the white scars along my temples faded to brown,
I realized that breaking the bonds of my hair
insulted the creative genius of God.

My hair is a spiritual, sensual, regenerative life force--
the curls embrace my fingers like an affectionate lover.

I set out on a mission with stacks of *Essence* at my side—
the expert on
Saving Our Strands
from stress and scientific options.

Decrease and de-grease became my mantra
Live well
Healthy diet
Wholesome carbohydrates
Whole grains
Fruits and vegetables.

Pages and pages of cornrows
braids extending past the shoulders.

Still, beauty is conditional:

Avoid applying direct heat
Black hair is more delicate than people realize
If done too tight,
and worn over long periods
hair coming out at the root
possible circle-shaped balding.

Fragility of Black hair turned out to be a lie.
As I cycled through
braids, double-stranded twists,
afros wrapped under kente cloth, and cornrows
my hair's resilience taught me
the weakness was in my self-pride.
Keeping my hair natural is a labor of love.

I've been asked why,
told I'm not attractive being my original self.

However, I figure that
a brother who can't
relish nestling his fingers in the curls
just ain't deep.
Any sister who stares at me contemptuously
must learn the art of self-love.

As my hair is at its roots, so it shall be to the ends.

A Period Piece

Innocence interrupted one July
at age twelve.
Menarche

Finding blood,
I confided in my mother, who smiled
as I cried in her arms.

She ushered me into
secret cold-water washings
and discreet disposals in paper bags
so as not to offend Daddy.
He was mystified,
uncertain of how to comfort.

Blood coursing down, soaking,
so I'd stand,
sitting meant gushing

Cramping, writhing, bloating, headaches.

Craving sweetness to combat bitterness
but gobbling goodies only invites
cramping, bloating, headaches.

I adapt to my new "friend"
learn to mask blue moods that only I comprehend
and hide tears over stubborn pimples
thick glasses
my unreturned phone calls to Chris
and our breakup.

A girl wonders why, with this
bleeding prelude to birthing
pain must be part of the equation.

Gone are the days
when woman was Goddess, and
Menstrual blood was red magic.
In our menstrual huts
we communed with Mother Moon.

Catharsis comes from my fellow sufferers—
Mother, sister, aunts, cousins, sister-friends, through
womanly whispered sympathies and nods.
Companionship breeds synchronization.

At age twenty-one
my usual monthly calendar countdowns,
well-timed, suddenly are not.
I count and recount the days, to no avail.

Anxious anticipation, dread
Unabated fear and pointless prayers
Confirmation of my suspicions inexplicably brings joy.

I caress the growing life in my womb
Massaging my stretching, itching skin with cocoa butter
Stretch marks appear anyway.
I don't care.

Nine months later
moaning, heaving, retching, pushing, cursing, crying

a bleeding prelude to birthing
and then, my son.

Along the oft-confusing way
my mother, aunts, sister, and sister-friends
through womanly sympathies and nods
help me navigate this womanly journey.

All along, I've wondered about
this bleeding prelude to birthing.
That blushing girl of twelve
has grown in her red understanding
about this bloody revenge for
Eve's alleged
shamelessness.

It is said in Leviticus 15
If a woman has issue
And her issue in her flesh be blood
She shall be put apart
Put apart
put apart for seven days
Whosoever touches her
Or her bed
Shall be unclean

If any man be with her at all
And her flowers upon him
He shall be unclean

Banished to *their* menstrual huts
during each bleeding prelude to birthing
we sang our red river stories, still
meditating off the strength of our
sacred blood red wounds.

One day
I'm gonna build me a menstrual hut
where we rebel women,
amongst frankincense and myrrh,
will sip ginger or peppermint tea
sing
sacred red river stories
dance nude on ruddy nights
and invite our brothers to
sacred surrender.
When they've fallen into crimson dreams
we'll gather our sisters through our womanly whispers.

We moon-mothers,
daughters of Isis,
Diana,
Kali
will paint ourselves
in red ochre
douse towering trees with red dew
slaughter the war-god,
and resurrect the Goddess.

V

The Invitation

Under the stroke of your hand,
I am dewy.
My flesh plumps like a muscadine.

I see love
in the onyx pools of your eyes.

Come on, and
slip into something
comfortable.

Troubled Mind

In my uneasy dreams
You're standing above me
Surrounded by the glow of candlelight
Your penis a swinging pendulum
Before my eyes

I'm dumbfounded, transfixed
by old memories
of you and me, locked in tight embrace
struggling
to hold on to sanity
in the hazy world of orgasm

We kept coming and screaming
coming and moaning
coming and sighing
coming and smiling

But you thought one way, I thought another.

So we ended up going
(for a little while)

but loneliness is a bitch

and it wouldn't be long
before I'd salvage your number from the trash
and run to the solace of your arms

Then we'd talk
argue
scream
and be back to the coming and going

It took so long before I realized
that what felt so much like love
was really lust in disguise

I must have been hypnotized

Sweet Georgia Brown

Soft-spoken lover
Gifted with great imagination, insight, sensitivity
An infectious, impulsive spirit
Free and wild as the wind, but
Not unwilling to share intimacy

You've wrapped me in a cloak of blackness and kept me warm
Your every stroke of my hair is an affirmation
Your gaze on me is a soft, luminous spotlight

I feel like a nubile goddess, a precious find

I love to watch you undress
The sight of your lean, naked body is an aphrodisiac
Skin like brown sugar
Penetrating, soulful ebony-onyx eyes
Arching neck, sloped back

Our lovemaking is a hot steamy wet dream
I don't want to awaken from
You must have stolen into the recesses of my mind
Seen my innermost desires and discovered all my soft spots.

When we're on that physical plane—
And believe me, it's quite a ride—
We're mellow, sensuous music:
The riffs of jazz
The passion of soul
The psychedelic ecstasy of rock and roll
Rock and roll
Rock and roll
You rock and roll your hips gently, gently
Coaxing me
Making us sweat a hundred babbling brooks
Making me moan and heave
You, waxing poetic: exquisite, heavenly, divine
Until we hit the boundary of pleasure
And explode.

It doesn't stop there, because you hold me.
We laugh, we talk, or fall off to sleep, arms intertwined, spirits in sync.
There's nothing casual about this sex.
You make me feel the way a woman should,
Sweet Georgia Brown.

Ineptitude

Sister Gloria, I said,
as I climbed onto her porch

Help me
I was down by the water
walking
and
I was bitten by a snake

She leaned forward on her rocking chair
examined the wound, and smiled

Most likely, it was a cottonmouth

It's just a dry bite

it usually ain't lethal

but you better be careful
'cause they could be venomous

If you ever see another
she said,

"Check its mouth
when it opens wide"

Resurrection of a Poet
(for J.A.)

Thanks brother

Your deep
        deep
                poems

make music of mundanities.

My inner rhythms quickened, and
I realized how long it had been
since I had written anything at all.

I thought,
Well, damn.
No wonder I had been unhappy.

So even though you left
and I haven't heard
or read
a word from you,

We've spoken.

Yeah, we have, 'cause
I internalized your creative spirit
it meshed with mine,
and my words have been flowing like the river Nile
ever since.

Who said brothers can't be beautiful?

And just think
you probably never suspected
you'd be the reason for
the resurrection of a poet.

Thabiti

His deep voice resonates
those pensive ebony eyes
draw me in
and embrace me.

His lips evade description
except they are full
and I want to caress them with mine.

Thoughts of him
conjure images of a panther
cool
black
exuding a proud aura
that could be mistaken for arrogance
but
he is a humble man before God.

His intelligence,
his spirituality intrigues me
his sexual passions await exploration
beneath his cool exterior.

I dream of him, often

My feelings for him
are a mystery to me
love
obsession
infatuation
lust

Only time will reveal.

A Senryu

Enthralled, I forgot
to blow curls of steam off your
passion. It burned my mouth.

A Deux

He asked me if I wanted company, and I,
yearning, said,
Come.

He sat on my sofa.
He laid on my bed.
In a fit of loneliness,
I invited his touch.
Rub my back, I asked.
I've been told I'm good at massages, he said.

Someone lied.

I surrendered anyway,
simply glad to be underneath a man's hands.

It was nice, at first.
And then he pulled me to him, roughly.

He was a loose fit, like baggy jeans.
I changed my mind, but
don't know where no went.

He was finished before I began,
my disappointment, his surprise.

We fell asleep, fitfully.

He rushed out at sunrise
purpose, fulfilled.

I washed away his scent with lavender soap,
laundered the sheets, remade the bed
and tossed the condom wrapper in the trash.
But still
his touch wrapped itself inside my memory,
and settled in my soul like a patina of dust.

Choice is God's greatest gift.

Victim

Perfumed and laced, I
waited on the bed for you.
The phone never rang
with an excuse on the other end.

I began to think about how we met
when I was young and thought
my life a meandering yawn,
and I loved
a man who named me
Plan B.

Your laughter bouncing off my walls
convincing caresses,
and instructive thrusts,
my heart opened wide.
So did my ears,
to the dark corners of your past
when you stalked feminine
innocence and desperation.
I loved you still.

I went outside for fresh air,
to contemplate
this human need to hurt--
children upon anthills
dictators upon dissenters--
and
in the parking lot
the slow brown movement
of a baby turtle
caught my eye.

It was alone
craning its neck
left to right
with its tentative steps
toward a world of
towering buildings and
fast cars driven by scurrying people.
There are few patches of grass here
free from the thud
of hard-soled human feet.

I took note of its position
and as I drove away
I made a wide swerve.

MYOPIA: A Pantoum

Men don't have the words for such eyes—
The ones I see when I look in the mirror
They're small, a non-descript brown when seen indoors
But my eyes are amber in sunlight

The eyes I see when I look in the mirror
Men don't look in my eyes for long
But my eyes are amber in sunlight
Other parts catch their attention.

Men don't look in my eyes for long
They're small, a non-descript brown when seen indoors
Other parts catch their attention
Men don't have the words for such eyes.

"I want to suck your titties"
"You have a nice ass"
"Open your legs"
"You need to give me that pussy"

"You have a nice ass".
Perhaps they lack the words to express what they see
"You need to give me that pussy".
I'll teach the next man new vocabulary

Perhaps they lack the words to express what they see
I'll teach the next man new vocabulary.
"Open your legs"
"I want to suck your titties"

Sex masqueraded as love
Why do they always close their eyes (so I can't see)?
I want the next man to see my soul.
I learned sex without love is empty.

Why do they always close their eyes (so I can't see)?
I used to be nearsighted
I learned sex without love is empty
I got new glasses

I used to be nearsighted
I want the next man to see my soul
I got new glasses
I will refuse sex masqueraded as making love.

A Song For You

Today I saw a film about space

In total darkness
I gaped
at the stars and planets
on the domed ceiling
the narrator relaying the story of
eons ago when Earth was young
a great mass collided with her
emitting giant chunks of rock.
Over time, the moon was born

I thought of our cosmic dance
of eons ago
when
you challenged my worldviews
cooked me breakfast
told jokes that made me laugh
your bedroom window had no curtains
you washed my back
got wet when you were dry
and
how I liked the way
you liked the way I looked
nude
in the moonlight.

Then there was the day
we went to the mall.
You bought me a teddy
brown
soft
with a poem
wrapped in golden wire
gently suggesting we could grow in love.

So when you confessed
to loving her still
a primordial scream
erupted from my throat.

I dreamed of encircling my hands around your neck
and squeezing
yet
if given the chance
I would have forgotten
and kissed your unwilling lips.

As time passed
the pieces of my heart melded together
I loved and lost, then loved again
as have you.

I smile about you now

Sometimes when I'm alone at night
I draw my blinds open wide
and stand nude
in the moonlit glow at my window

Beatitude

he came with more
mealy-mouthed promises

i told him to
go home

when he asked me why

i just said

for the same reason
i don't mix
splenda
or nutrasweet
in my
lemonade
carrot cake
or chocolate mousse

he said
i don't get it

i smiled
and said
i know

Anike

As she models her
brand new brand name
dress
in the mirror,

I watch.

She gives her chocolate brown
kinky twists
a toss
so her hair can fly.

She spins
to feel the wisp of cool air
against her butterscotch skin

She smiles
and calls herself
the cutest girl in the world.

Shielding my eyes
from her sparkling aura
I shake my head
and my index finger

Stop that, I say
Thinking modesty is noble.

But then again,
As I look at my life
I am glad my niece believes.

Maybe she won't end up
with her self-esteem all black and blue.

The Anteroom

Baby I must tell you
I can't be the type
to eat
a plum, or a
peach,
or an apple
before it's ripe.

Though you desire my dainty meats,
a pure heart and motive is what I seek.

Love is more than honeyed lickings,
strawberry cream,
and appetent sighs

I do want you
but caress my thoughts before my thighs.
Fondle my aspirations,
my breasts won't disappear.
The small of my back can wait,
knead my doubts and fears.

Explore my world.
Then, take me to heaven.

Baggage Claim

Old loves,
split ends.
For healthy growth,
cut them off.

VI

Fortune Cookie

Although I am in a rush, I am stopped
by my reflection in the windows of
the subway cars.
I'm wearing my woe--
no makeup
dull complexion
dumpy clothes
scuffed sneakers
impossibly long coat
shaping my body into a lowercase "l".

Sandra walks by me
and
three men turn their heads in her direction.
One mutters,
Yeah, I *like* that.

Her hair highlighted
in nuances of brown, blunt cut.
Fire-red coat,
black knee-high boots, and
her pain
tucked neatly into the pockets
of her tight black jeans.

I am twelve years younger than she
and no one would know.

I slide into a seat next to her
we laugh and chat
about our kids
money
jobs
hell,
just being a woman
is work.

On the way to my school,
I reach into my pocketbook for a tissue,
pull out an old paper from a fortune cookie instead.

People rely on your dependability.

I smile sadly at
lessons planned
classes taught
tissues
band-aids
sympathy
paper, pens and pencils distributed
and unreturned
directions explained 10 times 10
five essays revised simultaneously
spit out the gum
that is the rule
and because I said so
homework graded
bulletin boards filled

books read and reread

home on the train
standing on throbbing feet most of the way

son retrieved
homework asked for and checked
dinners cooked
school meetings
lights out, for him.

Then there is me
wild hair
sore back
rattling knees
bulging belly.
This baby fat is no excuse—
he is now thirteen.

I am in Barnes and Noble.
Walking past the yoga equipment,
a young Indian woman
draped in reds, oranges, yellows
and black flowing hair
smiles
from a DVD cover--
"boogie to the bhangra beat".
I get home and pop it in.

She says smile, and I do,
through the muscle strain.

She invites me to shimmy my hips.
I stretch out my stiffness
flutter my arms like a butterfly
swing
my legs open and shut
in coordinated motion
inhale my funky perspiration
and love it.

I went to a salon.
A sister from Africa
steamed, exfoliated, and moisturized my face
massaged my scalp as she gently washed my hair
wishing hers as thick as mine.

When she was done with my new curly 'fro
she begged me not to put on my glasses
she spun me around to face the mirror
and exclaimed
look
you're beautiful.

Solitude

Awed by the ocean's wholeness
that could swallow me up,
I squish my toes in wet sand as
crashing waves of jade
collide into my thighs.

The receding water reflects sunlight
like a cache of jewels.

A day fit for a queen.

Pathways

Son, if you ever hit
a patch of black ice

You have to let God
Right your vehicle

If you try to steer
You'll spin out

A Woman's Wisdom
(To Virginia J.)

I know
it is futile to
wish
I could crumble
my pain
and throw it away
like a paper ball.

Absence of memory
is death.

What I will do now
is blow the dust
off the hopes and dreams
I set aside
so my spirit can soar.

And knowing
that opening my mouth
is the same as opening my heart,
I will
look and listen more
speak a little less
and
draw my line in the sand

Truth
(for Acacia)

even though

my pot has no lid

I still cook

the flavors

take longer to mingle

but

my food is

warm

spicy

satisfying

Homegoing

Daddy, propped in bed, eyes open
surrounded by our grateful embrace
laughing, talking
the forest green casket empty
his funeral a distant dream.

"Where'd you have me?"
"Calverton," I said.
Daddy hung his head.
"I'm sorry, I'm sorry", I mumbled,
and awakened.

Calverton Cemetery, honoring his time fixing planes
during the war in Vietnam, took him for free
and it was not the place he wanted to be.

Daddy wanted to be buried with his grandparents
in Hassel, North Carolina
underneath the big tree in that
small-gated graveyard
adjacent to fields of
purple-flowered cotton and peanuts.

After that dream
I decided to send him home.

Searching for a proper way,
I came across the *Dama* of
Mali's Dogon people who
located Sirius B with naked eyes.

Months of picking and choosing
amongst their traditions and language
knowing in my rush, I was oversimplifying
hoping they'd forgive me
for my dearth of ancestral memory.

I gathered sanseviera fibers
to be weaved into red and black anklets and bracelets.
Imported pollo trees, planted them in the courtyard.
After they reached a certain height
nights found me
sawing shaving sanding,
sculpting painting wood
carving blades for the sirige masks.

Sick of slipping on wood splinters,
awakening to thunderous echoes of late-night drums,
my neighbors had a meeting about me.

When I told them about the Dama
they stared at me, shook their heads
and took my red/black/yellow stained hands in theirs.

Girl, we far away from Mali
and he's gone, you gotta move on.

Yes, I said, my grief is two years long,
yet it's the Dogon way.
I gotta get him home.

One Sunday morning
I stood in the green field behind my building
surrounded by the masks of cows
birds, and antelopes.

I banged on the bui-na drum
'til I saw faces pop in windows.

An elder approached,
and studied my steady tears.

Understanding,
he lifted the drum from my hands
and cried out

Wo! (come)
Hear my *yanda* (call)
We must bring our fathers to their *damma* (country)
Hear my *pili* (song)

Boys and men of all ages
began to gather

I motioned towards the masks
and they put them on

We began to walk

Wo!
Hear my *yanda*
We must bring our fathers to their damma
Hear my *pili*

Upon seeing the terrible masks
children hid their faces
but the women--
the women
lined the streets
and got to clapping

When we got to Harlem
deacons and preachers began to stream into line
and they began to call

Wo!
Hear my yanda
We must bring our fathers to their damma
Hear my pili

Hours later
at Daddy's grave
The Elder drummed louder
The masks began their terrible dance

The sirige masks came forth
Moving forwards and backwards
Blades scratching the ground
East and west, in imitation
of Creation

After hours they knelt
facing east

The Elder came forth
Dee!
Wo!
We're going to send you home!

Daddy arose, bathed in white aura.

The drumming grew louder
the Elder tapped my shoulder
and pointed to the approach of
millions of Black men
bathed in white aura.

They gathered 'round.
The Elder smiled.

We marched to the Rockaways
and faced the Atlantic
the masks, in their terrible dance
the women clapping and singing

The Elder and spirits stepped forth

Dee!
When you get there,
shine on the black faces of the pharaohs
as they come to light.
Look over the shoulders of our scholars
in Ibadan and Timbuktu.
Nurture the seeds of democracy planted throughout Africa.
Wrap your arms
around the children of Soweto and
refugees of Somalia, Sudan, and the Congo.
Make rain upon the lands of Ethiopia,
fertilize her soil.
Disarm the warlords!
Rejuvenate her industries!
Help our brothers and sisters rebuild our home!

Daddy and the other spirits joined hands
and began their journey across the Big Water.

The masks in their terrible dance
the women, ululating
me, crying.

For six days we went on.

One by one, the dancers left the circle

and when the sun set
the Elder nodded at me
and said,
It is done.

Sunset

First memory:
holding Daddy's hand
skipping alongside
coming home from our god-sister Crystal's house
after Mommy gave birth to a
beautiful chubby-cheeked baby
with silky black hair I envied.

We were Carla and Donna.
Spoke and laughed in unison.
Jumped on our beds,
challenged Daddy to pillow fights
in the bedroom we shared in Apartment 8B.
Cooked each other fake meals with our play kitchen set.
Played African Village at bath time.
Stirred our play soup with the back brush.
Splashed in the tub until all the bubbles popped.
Play doh. Crayons and coloring books.
Took turns spinning ourselves sick on our Sit and Spin.

Blinking blue/green/yellow/red lights on Christmas eves.
We'd beckon daybreak,
nudge Mommy and Daddy awake
for the ripping of packages with perfect bows from
them, Nana, Pop-Pop, Grandma, and our aunts and uncles.

Criss-crossing fingers braided the hair of our styling heads.
Mouths puckered, cheeks puffed out blowing breath/life
into inflatable dollhouse furniture.
Water splashing in the play pool we had for our dolls so they could swim.
Sat on the floor, knees touching.
Josie and the Pussycats. Magilla Gorilla.
Fat Albert. Bugs Bunny. Heckle and Jeckle. The Jackson 5ive.
Checkers/backgammon/Parcheesi.

Spring/summer/fall was the slamming of the screen door,
sweating out our cornrows or press-n-curls.
Big Wheels speeding, crushing gravel.
Hula hoops rotating our hips like Saturn's rings.
Red-light-green light 1-2-3, roller skates, kickball.
Bike riding all around the block
and through the house when Mommy and Daddy were out.

Piano/flute/ballet at Harlem School of the Arts.
Squeals of, Daddy, please?
Read to Ms. Mulzac at Liberation Bookstore with polysyllabic ease.
Got lost in Virginia Hamilton. Alice Childress. Walter Dean Myers.
Cinnamon rolls at Better Pie Crust.
Sticky fingers against wax paper.

Giggled our way to North Carolina.
Played with Aunt Bea and Uncle Reuben's neighbor children
until the porch lights came on/lightning bugs were out.
In bed, stared at each other through southern-style darkness,
spooked by the crickets, missing New York noise.

Recited Rappers Delight and made up our own—
she was Lady Dee and rocked viciously.

I was bossy big sister who reprimanded Mommy and Daddy
for letting Donna cry her way out of eating vegetables.
Cleaned her room when it wasn't neat enough.
Ran up to her with the ugliest pictures of bugs in our encyclopedias:
"Donna, look!"
Laughed through her screaming,
tried to hug her quiet before the leather belt swung my way.
She tortured me too, singing "All I Want for Christmas Is My Two Front Teeth".

Still, we made popcorn.
Underneath Mommy's afghans, we
kicked each other's thighs under the cover.
Watched Star Wars. Claudine. Mommie Dearest.

Shared my room/secrets at Spelman.
Cheered our commencements.

She gathered Khari in her arms; best buddies since.
When she gave birth to Anike, I chose her middle name
and slept on the floor until the nurse put me out.
Hours on the phone unraveling mysteries of motherhood/men/
missing Daddy/all the relatives who transitioned.
Watched "The Chappelle Show", "Mad TV", "Mad Men", "Queen Sugar",
"Insecure".

Before the GPS, we were one great driver!

Donna,
the Nettie to my Celie,
hand-clapping and screaming, "Write!"

I hope I held her hand enough.

Donna,
The clink and shine of new coins
the purple streak in a rainbow
sun rays breaking through clouds
North Star sparkle
moonlit gleam on the bay.

Southern Lullaby

Summers found us rolling for hours until we hit
stealthy North Carolina heat.

After hugging Uncle Reuben
and running past
his sky-blue Lincoln Town Car

into the kitchen
awash
in pork salt scent,
I wrapped long skinny arms around her waist.

Aunt Bea,
I said,
What are we gonna eat?

She, with silky silver hair
coaxed into a bun,
face crinkled into a gentle smile,
sang
"gnat feathers and butterfly wings."

VII

Mama Afrika

This ain't no tall tale.
It's the true story,
of the wisest woman in the world,
Mama Afrika.

It had been yet another disappointing meeting for the New Men of the Millennium. Hakeem and the rest of the brothers had expected at least fifty men to come out, and only three had shown up. They had spent the last four hours debating about what to do to attract more men to the organization.

Hakeem couldn't wait to get home and go to bed after another late night. Between work, school, and the group, he hardly slept.

He suddenly felt a heavy hand on his shoulder and tensed immediately.

"Yo, what's up my nigga?" It was Rob.

Hakeem smiled wearily and as he gave him a pound and a quick hug. "What's up? What you doin' out here?"

"Nothin' man, you know me," Rob replied. He gestured towards the corner.

"Hey bro', you know there's nothin' out here for you," Hakeem began. "You thought any more about joining the group?"

"Aw man, that's bullshit. A bunch of broke-ass niggas sittin' around talking about how fucked up the community is. I don't need to go to a fuckin' meeting to know that. I'm out here every night so I know what's going on in these streets. Fuck that."

"Rob, we don't just talk about what's happening in the streets, but we talk about how to make good things happen."

Rob laughed. "What ya'll gon' do? You gon' help a brother get paid?"

Hakeem sighed. "Eventually. It takes time. We have to teach the young brothers to stop selling drugs, stay out of prison, get an education, and develop entrepreneurial skills…"

Hakeem reached into his bag for a copy of Haki Madhubuti's *Black Men: Obsolete, Single, Dangerous?* "Yo man, read this."

Rob waved him off. "I heard all that shit before. "He looked off at his boys, and the stream of cars that began to stop near them. He reached out to give Hakeem a pound.

"Yo, I'm out. Peace, my nigga!"

Hakeem watched Rob saunter away. "We're not niggas," he said, knowing Rob couldn't hear him.

He sagged against a brick wall and put his head in his hands.

He stood there for a moment, until he sensed a presence lurking nearby. He looked up in time to see a shadowy figure approach. He started to walk away.

"Hey youngblood," the figure whispered as he came into the light from the streetlamp. "I know what you're looking for."

Hakeem turned to face the man. "What?"

The man stepped closer and looked up at Hakeem. Once Hakeem saw the nervous tic and bloodshot eyes, he knew who it was.

"Oh 'Fess, it's you. You scared me, man."

"I see you, man. I know you trying to do the right thing, and these young heads out here can't hear the wisdom of your words. You can't handle this alone. The black man's problems are too heavy for one man's shoulders.

He whispered, "You need Mama Afrika."

Hakeem was puzzled. "Who?"

"Mama Afrika," the man replied.

"She was an organizer, a teacher, and a healer. Man, she could make things around here good again."

"Where did she go?"

'Fess inched closer until he was right underneath Hakeem's nose. "Mama Afrika is magical. You only need to do two things to find her."

"What would I have to do?"

'Fess smiled. "First you have to believe that there is hope for Black Power. Second, you have to stand on your rooftop, and call for her."

Hakeem glared at 'Fess. "People are going to think I'm crazy if I'm standing on my roof screaming for Mama Afrika. They'll lock me up!"

"Do you believe that the situation is desperate enough? Over a million black men in prison, thousands of brothers are unemployed, most Black children are born into single parent homes, and thousands of people infected with AIDS."

"Yeah, yeah, man I know all of that. But how is Mama Afrika going to help?"

'Fess smiled mysteriously and turned to walk away.

"Why don't you call Mama Afrika?"

'Fess disappeared into the night.

Hakeem stared after 'Old 'Fess, remembering the neighborhood stories about Professor John Strong, scholar and community leader. He had run a school with other neighborhood activists, where they taught black history and literature, art, African dance and drumming. They ran seminars about dealing with the police and had job training programs. The neighborhood had been like a family.

Like so many other Black activists, Professor Strong found himself under the surveillance of COINTELPRO. Constantly on the lookout for agent provocateurs and terrified by the killings, he eventually was driven mad.

Mama Afrika must be another figment of his imagination, Hakeem thought. He pulled his coat tighter around his body and walked toward his building.

Hakeem jumped up from his bed with a start. A noise had awakened him. He reached over for the lamp and turned it on. There was broken glass on the floor and a small hole in the window. Suddenly, he heard three loud pops. He quickly dove to the floor by his bed.

A woman was screaming outside, and a car alarm was going off.

Hakeem waited to make sure that there weren't any more shots, and he rushed out of his room into his mother's. "Mama!"

She was sitting on her bed in the dark.

"Are you OK, Mama? Did you hear the shots?"

"Yes". She began rocking back and forth. "I'm so tired."

"What's wrong?"

She sobbed. "Why can't there ever be any peace around here?"

Hakeem hugged her. He didn't even know what to say. So many times he assured her that he and his brothers and sister would find a way to buy a house in a nice neighborhood. Most times that aspiration seemed like an unattainable dream.

A surge of anger overcame him, and he rushed out of the room.

"Hakeem!"

He didn't stop to face his mother but ran out of the apartment. He ran up the stairs, two at a time, until he reached the rooftop. He flung the metal door open and screamed.

"Mama Afrika!"

As his voice rang out, all the neighborhood noises—police sirens, passing cars that blasted music loud enough to be felt inside of apartments—ceased.

Hakeem listened to the silence, and it enraged him even more.

"Mama Afrika! Mama Afrika! Where are you? I hate this fuckin' neighborhood! Nobody gives a damn! Mama Afrika!"

Hakeem, thoroughly exhausted, sat down on the ledge. He looked out over the bright lights of the city and the sparkling skyscrapers in the distance. He smiled as he remembered the days when he and Rob would make grandiose plans of buying big houses and telling their mothers to quit working.

He wiped away his tears and headed back downstairs.

****

Hakeem awoke with a start. Eight o'clock. He'd be late for his African History class. He jumped in the shower, cleaned up, and dressed. As he opened the door to leave, there was a woman standing there.

She was tall and straight-backed, with dark penetrating eyes, cocoa-colored skin and locks that same color hanging down her back.

"You called me?"

Hakeem was entranced. "Who are you?"

She smiled as she moved inside his apartment. "I am Mama Afrika. Tell me what you need."

****

'Fess had been right. Things were changing ever since Mama Afrika had been going around the streets talking to the people, giving hugs and advice. Mama Afrika was unafraid. She talked to the drug dealers, the kids running the streets, the homeless. Everyone.

The young brothers were still hanging out on the corners, but they were discussing Malcolm X, the Panthers, The Last Poets, and the community programs they wanted to start with the New Men of the Millennium. The drug buyers had stopped coming around the block and there hadn't been a shooting in weeks. More children were seen hanging out with their fathers. More kids were going to school. They were still disrupting class, but only to ask why the ancient Egyptians still looked white in their textbooks and why they didn't learn about black mathematicians. Hakeem could not believe all the changes that had taken place over the last year. Even his mother stopped talking about moving away, and she began a community garden.

Word began to get out. Newspapers ran stories about Mama Afrika's turnaround of the neighborhood. Community groups from California, Florida, Washington D.C, and Texas all began to ask for Mama Afrika.

Hakeem was not surprised when Mama Afrika came to him one day and laid her hand on his shoulder.

"It is time for me to go. I lit the spark, and the rest of you must stoke the fire."

"Mama Afrika, thank you."

The next night she was gone.

****

It did not take long for things to fall apart. Interest in all the books Mama Afrika told people to read began to wane. The dealers were tired of being broke, and soon the buyers began to reappear in their cars. Shootings became commonplace, and people were discouraged.

Hakeem couldn't believe it. What had changed? What could be done?

They needed Mama Afrika.

Hakeem called her, and the next day, she reappeared at his doorstep. But she was not the same.

The running back and forth to meetings, the speeches, the counseling sessions, all had taken their toll. Mama Afrika had puffy bags underneath her eyes and her locs had begun to snap off. She looked bloated and sad.

Still, Hakeem was overjoyed by her presence.

"Mama," he exclaimed as he hugged her. "We've needed you."

"My brother, I am tired."

"Mama Afrika, I don't know what to do. I'm afraid. The violence, the drugs, the apathy have all returned since you left."

Mama Afrika sat down despairingly on the sofa. "Hakeem, do you know how hard it is to try and save the world? I have been to Oakland and Phoenix and Houston and Harlem and everywhere it is the same. Our brothers and sisters are looking to me to save them."

Hakeem was frightened by the resignation on Mama Afrika's face. "Mama, have you given up? If you give up, I don't know what I'll do."

Mama Afrika looked up at Hakeem. He was so young, and he cared. He had the one gift that could save them all—hope. There was one thing that she could do.

She pulled Hakeem down to her, and stared into his eyes. "Hakeem, spread the word. Have everyone come down to the courtyard next Friday night. Tell them that I have the answer to all the ills we suffer as a people. Tell them that if they want my help they must come and see me."

Hakeem smiled. "I will."

Mama rose to go. There was much work to be done.

******

There was a crowd, five thousand strong. Everyone lined the blocks around Hakeem's building and stared anxiously at the makeshift stage that volunteers had quickly constructed. Excitement was in the air. Mama Afrika was back! They all wondered what miracle she was to perform.

A murmur rushed through the crowd. A round figure appeared on the dais. It was Mama Afrika! She was summoning a few dozen men to carry baskets up on the stage. Cheers resounded throughout the neighborhood.

Mama! Mama! Mama!

She approached the microphone, and a hush washed over the crowd. They leaned forward to hear her speak.

"Brothers and sisters, I greet you in the spirit of love! It has been a while since I was last here. Our brother Hakeem called me because the great progress we made during our time together has disappeared. He asked me to help."

Mama gestured to her assistants to pass around the baskets.

"The baskets that are being passed around have gifts for all of you. In each box there is the answer to solving all our community's ills. Please do not open it until I say the word."

It took over an hour for each person to get his or her box, and they waited patiently for Mama to give the word. When all the baskets returned to Mama empty, she nodded.

"I love you all." She waved and walked off the stage.

The people opened their boxes, and they were like kids at Christmas. Cries of disappointment began to ring out, followed by outbursts of anger.

"Yo, what the fuck? I waited an hour for this?!!?"

Hakeem felt panicky. What had Mama Afrika done? Quickly he opened his own box. He was shocked when he saw his own reflection.

Afterword

Although the title of *Gnat Feathers and Butterfly Wings* was born out of my joyful memory of my beloved Aunt Beatrice's humorous way of chasing me out of her kitchen so she could finish cooking, this collection had its genesis in grief.

My father died from multiple myeloma in 2005, and I did not handle it well. I developed an eating disorder that made me sick, and I was determined to find another way to channel my anger and sadness. One day I happened to pick up my copy of my cousin Alice Witt-Smith's book *Up Close and Personal,* that she had given to me at Daddy's wake, and read it. Impressed, I thought about my own poetry and thought to myself, *maybe I should do that.*

I got busy. I gathered old notebooks from high school and college, compiled the poems, and selected the ones worthy of revision. I attended poetry workshops led by Jacqueline Johnson and Cecily Parks, and a Creative Writing class with Sheree Renee Thomas, where my story "Mama Africa" was born. I began writing new poems about my family, relationships, socio-political issues, current events, and my love of jazz music. I got the courage to submit my poem "Anike" that I wrote for my niece for publication, and *Anderbo* published it under the title "Niece". With that acceptance under my belt, I chose to self-publish my book under Wasteland Press in 2008.

Thank you for joining me on this journey through my late teens through my early thirties. I hope you enjoyed these snippets of my heart and soul.

The Author

Carla M. Cherry is a native of the Bronx, NY. A graduate of Spelman College, New York University, and Lehman College, she has been teaching in the New York City public schools since 1996. Her poetry has appeared in various publications, including Anderbo, Eunoia Review, Dissident Voice, Random Sample Review, Firefly Magazine, Picaroon Poetry, Streetlight Press, MemoryHouse, Bop Dead City, Ariel Chart, Anti-Heroin Chic, The Racket, and Raising Mothers. All five of her books of poetry were published by ii-Publishing, which includes: *Gnat Feathers and Butterfly Wings, Thirty Dollars and a Bowl of Soup, Honeysuckle Me, These Pearls Are Real*, and *Stardust and Skin*. She is an M.F.A. candidate in Creative Writing at the City College of New York.

CONNECT WITH ME:

Email: carla.cherrybxpoet@gmail.com
Website: www.carlacherrybxpoet1.com
Facebook: @poeticchic
Twitter: @carla_bronxpoet
Instagram: @carlabxpoet1

Publication Credits

Many of the poems in this collection originally appeared on Zathom.com, an online platform that gives its subscribed writers three fathoms (words or phrases) and challenges them to write a poem, story, or piece of nonfiction in 55 words or less.

The poems written on and for Zathom.com have the words that inspired them in bold print. If any of you are writers, I hope you'll be moved to use them in your own original poems!

"Anike" was originally published by anderbo.com under the title "Niece".

"Last Request" originally appeared in Ariel Chart.

"Black Pearl" originally appeared on Eric McPherson's CD Continuum.

"African Beauties" originally appeared in Synaeresis.

"You Gambled" was originally published by The Racket.

"Sunset" originally appeared in Interstice.

www.ingramcontent.com/pod-product-compliance
Lightning Source LLC
Chambersburg PA
CBHW071812080526
44589CB00012B/771